MUSTARD SEED
PREACHING

Ann M. Garrido

Catechesis of
the Good Shepherd
Publications

MUSTARD SEED PREACHING © 2004 Archdiocese of Chicago: Liturgy Training Publications, 1800 North Hermitage Avenue, Chicago IL 60622-1101; 1-800-933-1800, fax 1-800-933-7094, e-mail orders@ltp.org. All rights reserved. See our website at www.ltp.org.

Catechesis of the Good Shepherd Publications is an imprint of Liturgy Training Publications (LTP). Further information about these publications is available from LTP or from the Catechesis of the Good Shepherd, PO Box 1084, Oak Park, IL 60304; 708-524-1210; fax 708-386-8032. Requests for information about other aspects of the Catechesis should be directed to this address.

This book was edited by Margaret Brennan. Carol Mycio was the production editor. The design is by Larry Cope, and the typesetting was done by Jim Mellody-Pizzato in Times Roman and Matrix. Cover illustration by Julie Lonneman/ thespiritsource.com.

Printed in the United States of America.

Library of Congress Control Number: 2004111883

ISBN 1-56854-555-X

CGSMS

MUSTARD SEED
PREACHING

Other Catechesis of the
Good Shepherd Publications

Living Liturgy
Sofia Cavalletti

The Religious Potential of the Child
Sofia Cavalletti

The Religious Potential of the Child 6 to 12 Years Old
Sofia Cavalletti

The Good Shepherd and the Child: A Joyful Journey
Sofia Cavalletti, Patricia Coulter, Gianna Gobbi, and
Silvana Q. Montanaro

History's Golden Thread: The History of Salvation
Sofia Cavalletti

The Catechesis of the Good Shepherd in a Parish Setting
Tina Lillig

A Is for Altar, B Is for Bible
Judith Lang Main

Journals of the Catechesis of the Good Shepherd, 1984–1997

Journals of the Catechesis of the Good Shepherd, 1998–2002

Discovering the Real Spiritual Life of Children (video)

CONTENTS

CONTENTS

FOREWORD

As a priest, I have been involved with the Catechesis of the Good Shepherd for some time. In the late 1970s, while serving at a Catholic parish in Oak Park, Illinois, I first met Lillian Lewis, a parishioner and seasoned lay ecclesial minister trained in the Catechesis of the Good Shepherd in its early years in Italy by the founder, Sofia Cavalletti, and one of the first to bring the Catechesis to North America. Another parishioner, Tina Lillig, is now director of the North American Association of the Catechesis of the Good Shepherd and was then my first catechist and ministerial colleague in the Catechesis. In 1983, I had the opportunity to meet Sofia Cavalletti, to become a charter member of the Association, and to do some initial training as a catechist with another leading North American catechist, Rebekah Rojcewicz.

From the beginning, I liked several things about being a priest in a Catechesis of the Good Shepherd parish:

- My appreciation of scripture and liturgy deepened in many ways, thanks to observing and participating with children and catechists in their catechetical work and prayer.

- As a preacher, my connection with both children and adults deepened as we contemplated the Gospel together.

- I prayed with dozens of amazingly faith-filled children and junior teens in preparation for and in celebration of the sacraments.

- I shared satisfaction with parents and other parishioners as our children grew and matured into young adults, living their faith actively in campus ministries and parishes and in many wonderful and diverse expressions of baptismal discipleship.

In the years following our first attempts at integrating the Catechesis at that parish, I watched the rapid expansion of the Catechesis in both Catholic and Protestant circles throughout Mexico, the United States, and Canada. Since coming to Aquinas Institute of Theology to teach preaching in 1994, I have watched the Catechesis take hold in parishes of St. Louis, and I have supported two doctor of ministry in preaching students as they were introduced to the Catechesis and did doctoral research on preaching with children.

Ann Mees Garrido, now my colleague as director of field education, placement, and parish relations at Aquinas Institute of Theology, was one of these students. With this book, you will have the pleasure of sharing Ann's insights— both as a catechist of the Good Shepherd at St. Francis Xavier College Church on the campus of St. Louis University and also as a Catholic lay theologian of remarkable substance.

Ann's book is directed to priests like myself and other ministers of the Word—catechists, Liturgy of the Word leaders, DREs, and deacons—who want to learn about the history, values, and vision of the Catechesis and discover how it can be a gift to their ministry. I recommend the book both to those serving currently in these ministries and also to those actively preparing for them, whether they currently employ the Catechesis of the Good Shepherd in their setting or not.

Ann talks early in this book about a "round trip" model of evangelization. Her experience as a college student on mission in Kenya, as a young Catholic school teacher in Guam, and now as a theological educator and a catechist of the Good Shepherd in her home city have made Ann one of that company of post–Vatican II missioners convinced that mission is essentially a dialogue: announcing the Great News (as children sometimes call it) to the poor, to the marginalized, and to Little Ones; entering into dialogue with them as they discover their own voice to praise God and to do theology vis-à-vis the Gospel meanings of their life; and letting this encounter come back home in new understandings and deepened faith in the life and world of the preacher/missioner.

We are called here to be Mustard Seed preachers, planting and nurturing the seeds and seedlings of faith in our children, in ourselves, and in our world. The reign of God is like the tiniest of seeds, and it will grow in us and in our world and in our cosmos until God is all in all. Please join me in accepting the invitation of this book: to listen with the little, to be a matchmaker between God and humanity and between daily life and the reign of God, to make of ourselves a sign that is congruent to the Gospel, and to preach the questions— preaching respectfully, essentially, beautifully, and joyfully.

Gregory Heille, OP
Director, Doctor of Ministry in Preaching
Aquinas Institute of Theology
St. Louis, Missouri

INTRODUCTION

The kingdom of God, Jesus said, is like a mustard seed—
"the smallest seed of all." If you have ever held one of these
tiny seeds on the tip of your finger, you know what he means.
Unlike their American counterparts, mustard seeds from the
land of Palestine are no larger than a fleck of pepper. And
yet, they grow to such a size that the "birds of the sky" come
to build nests in their branches. How could this be? How could
something this small carry such energy and power within it?
We can easily sympathize with the response of an elderly
woman who once shouted out as I preached, "That is ridiculous!" She suffered from Alzheimer's, but still possessed
particularly sharp eyesight, and could not conceive how
something so miniscule could result in something so great.

For those who engage in the ministry of preaching,
however, this is an act of trust that must regularly be made.
Preachers are confronted daily with the ridiculous, and not
only in Matthew 13:31–32. How can one talk for ten minutes
over an occasionally squealing microphone and hope that it
will capture peoples' imaginations more than the minute-by-
minute barrage of flashy words and images that compete on
the television and computer screen? How can one humble
person standing behind a pulpit make any difference at all?

Preaching is an act of faith in the kingdom of God, a conscious surrender to the hope that God could still do something great with mustard seed words.

This book is for preachers who know that they are small, but understand that smallness is no obstacle to God. It is for preachers who know the divine *modus operandi* always favors what appears impossible. It is for "mustard seed" preachers. The purpose of the book is to offer such preachers a theology that can sustain and enliven their hope and a theological community with whom they can continue to reflect upon it.

The source of the theology to which I refer is children. At first, this may seem puzzling: Isn't this the very population that is prone to drop kneelers to the ground during the homily and leave a trail of crushed Cheerios in the center aisle? Why would children's theology be particularly helpful to preachers? Can children even really think and speak about theological matters? If you have enjoyed significant time with children, however, you are probably already answering these questions for yourself with a smile. Children, you would agree, are natural theologians. While they do not undertake disciplined, systematic study of traditional textbooks, they do—in the terms of Anselm of Canterbury—possess great "faith," and a thousand questions to which they are "seeking understanding." Furthermore, while their particular life experience will be different from that of the preacher, this is a population that knows very well what it means to be small and hope in the power of God. As such, children's theology may have more to say to preachers' lives than was first imagined possible.

The theological community to which I refer is one that has done much over the past 50 years to encourage and facilitate children's theological reflection. The community is called the Catechesis of the Good Shepherd. The Catechesis is an international community of adults and children devoted to reflecting together upon the scriptures and liturgy of the Church, guided by the experiences and intuitions of the children. In many parishes and schools around this country, the Catechesis is being rapidly embraced as a powerful and effective means of forming the Church's youngest members in the faith. If you have ever visited an atrium, however, you may have sensed that the Catechesis of the Good Shepherd has an even larger mission. Its purpose is not only to educate the children in the Church; it is to educate the Church about the religious potential of children. It invites the whole Church to enjoy and consider the implications of children's reflection on the faith.

This book extends the invitation in a particular way to preachers. In doing so, it attempts to turn around a commonly asked question—How do we preach to children?—to instead ponder a larger and more foundational question: What do children have to teach us about preaching? The first chapter discusses how this latter question came to be and why it is so important for us to ask. The second chapter introduces the work of the Catechesis of the Good Shepherd and its method of living and exploring theological realities with children. The middle chapters of the book explore what we have learned through the Catechesis of the Good Shepherd about the questions that drive children's theology; the characteristics that shape it; and then, the theology itself—in essence, the particular synthesis of the Christian message as it is articulated by children. The closing chapters ponder what possibilities the above material has for our own "mustard seed" preaching both in terms of method and content.

Three communities of persons have been particularly influential and helpful in the shaping of this project and

I wish to thank them from the outset. The first is the community of the Catechesis of the Good Shepherd to which I have belonged for eight years—the children, their families, and my fellow catechists. I have been graced to find great wisdom here, but also the most profound of friendships. The second is the community of Aquinas Institute of Theology in St. Louis to which I have belonged for the same eight years. My relationship with the faculty, students, and staff has been marked by a different kind of wisdom, but the same quality of friendship. The last community is that of my extended family in which children have always been welcomed. I especially thank my husband, Miguel, who has endured and supported the "ridiculousness" of my particular ministerial call, and my son Micah, who has left behind many crushed Cheerios in his short life span but whose questions were the seeds from which this project evolved.

The Question

What do children have to teach us about preaching? The fact that we are able to entertain such a question says something about the impact of the Second Vatican Council on our lives. For several centuries before the Council, the ministry of the Church was perceived as a one-directional encounter. The ideal missionary was one who left on a ship to sail across the ocean and was not expected to return. The ideal teacher untiringly instructed students. The ideal preacher ardently prepared to share the message of the Gospel with the people in the pews. The Church recognized that it had a marvelous gift to share. It did not, however, expect to receive something in return. The Second Vatican Council adjusted the hinges on the door to the Church so that it could now swing both ways. The Church recognized that it not only had something to offer the many people of the world from various cultures, ages, and states of life; it had something to receive.

The awareness has had the most profound impact in the area of missiology. When our Church documents speak about evangelization of new cultures, they now talk about the importance of *inculturation*. They acknowledge that the Church must proclaim the Gospel in new cultures, but that the hearers are not passive listeners. While the Gospel transforms the culture, the culture also translates and embodies the Gospel in a new and distinctive way. The process of evangelization is not complete until the new culture is able to speak back its own embodiment of the Gospel for the Church to hear.

The testimony of modern-day missionaries has helped us to see how very important it is that this "speaking back" happens. When we are exposed to new theologies that emerge from settings other than our own, we begin to recognize how culturally conditioned our own expression of the faith is. We discover that there is more to God than we previously thought. There are new dimensions of the Gospel that we had not seen before. We find ourselves face to face with a Truth that is larger than any one culture's expression is able to capture. And, we realize that if we want to understand more fully the universal God proclaimed by the Church, we will need to listen to many different peoples' perspectives and experiences.

When these perspectives and experiences are voiced by those who come from the fringes of global society, we are coming to recognize that the "speaking back" becomes doubly important for the Church. The Church has a long history of valuing the insight of the poor and marginalized—a characteristic unique to the religious sphere. Unlike the political or economic spheres, the Church claims that it is not only the insights of the leaders and the learned that should be valued in a community, but also the insights of those considered the "least." This is not because the poor and marginalized are morally superior to others in society, but because they are the ones to whom the Gospel was first proclaimed by Christ. If we wish to truly understand the Gospel first announced to the *anawim* of Palestine, then we must sit beside and listen to this Gospel with their modern counterparts, and hear what it means to them. When the poor and the marginalized are able to "speak back" what they have heard, it is a gift to the whole

Church. We are able to glean a privileged perspective on our faith from those who were nearest to the heart of Jesus.

In the lives of many post–Vatican II missionaries, the work of listening has become as important as the work of proclaiming. They know they have a gift to offer. They recognize they also have a gift to receive—a gift that they must bring back to the community from which they came. Missionaries no longer purchase one-way tickets. For the sake of the whole Church, they know they must always make a round trip.

The "round trip" model of evangelization raises interesting questions for catechesis. Since the Second Vatican Council, a good amount of attention has been given to how we pass on our faith to children—an important and much-needed consideration. Far less consideration, however, has been given to catechesis as a two-way exchange. We must ask about the best way to teach and preach the Gospel to children. But, we must also ask, What do children have to teach us about the Christian message? Like any other group, children hear, translate, and embody the Gospel in a unique and distinctive way, shaped by their own experience. As such, they offer a perspective on the divine quite different from the perspective of adults—a view into the nature of God that we would not otherwise enjoy. Furthermore, children are clearly among those to whom Christ addressed the Gospel: "Let the little children come to me," he says. "The kingdom of God belongs to such as these" (Matthew 19:14), and, "I assure you, unless you change and become like little children, you will not enter the kingdom of God" (Matthew 18:3). These scriptures, like the Council, seem to suggest that we have something to receive from children. Unless we sit beside them and listen to the Gospel from their perspective, we will not enjoy the kingdom of God that Christ has come to proclaim. A particularly privileged perspective into this kingdom will be missing.

But, how do we minister among children in such a way that we both give and receive? How do we practice both proclamation and listening? How do we help children to "speak back" their insight into the Gospel for the rest of the Church to hear? Fifty years ago, an experiment of this sort was begun in Rome, by a Catholic woman named Sofia Cavalletti—an experiment that has come to be known as the Catechesis of the Good Shepherd. It is to this experiment that we will now turn.

THE CATECHESIS OF THE GOOD SHEPHERD

The origins of the Catechesis of the Good Shepherd are shrouded not so much in secrecy as in the fogginess of memory that surrounds profound, transformative moments disguised as everyday life. Just as it is difficult to trace the exact moment a mustard seed took root, Sofia Cavalletti admits, "We started without knowing we started."[1] Cavalletti (b. 1917), a scholar and translator of the Hebrew language and scriptures. She was also involved in several ecumenical and inter-religious committees, including the Vatican commission on Jewish–Christian relations. Somewhere in the spring of 1954, however, Cavalletti received a strange request. A close friend asked her to "do something" with her seven-year-old son in the way of religious education. Cavalletti resisted; she had no experience working with children. Her friend persisted, however, and eventually she agreed to meet the boy. Their initial two-hour discussion on the first page of Genesis intrigued Cavalletti: Why was the child so content, even joyful, to study scripture? Over the next several months, Cavalletti began to read the Bible with other children—not as a teacher would instruct her students, but as a co-listener with the children before the Word of God, and a co-wonderer about its meaning in their lives.

Cavalletti found a partner for her quest in the person of Gianna Gobbi. A former assistant to Maria Montessori, Gobbi introduced Cavalletti to the insight of Montessori, who had made similar observations about the religious potential of children earlier in the century. A woman ahead of her times, Montessori had accorded to children the kind of respect and reverence that modern missionaries attempt to observe when approaching a new culture. The pedagogy she developed sought to discover the children's questions and desires that motivated them to want to learn, rather than beginning with what adults wanted children to learn. Montessori had carefully created an educational environment that would help children to address their questions and meet their developmental needs through the use of hands-on materials, freedom of movement and choice of work, and intentional life in community. In this environment, the adult facilitated the educational experience but did not control it. Montessori believed that each child possessed an "Inner Teacher" who would guide the child toward what was most urgent for his or her self development.

Gobbi knew of Montessori's desire to apply her method to the religious formation of children. An active and outspoken Catholic, Montessori had believed that it was in this arena her pedagogical method would reach its fullest potential. She had begun exploring how this might take place as early as 1915 in one of her Spanish "Children's Houses"—an endeavor that she referred to as "the Barcelona Experiment"—but her efforts were sidetracked by the climate of war that engulfed her Italian homeland and her subsequent exile in India. Gobbi shared with Cavalletti some of the fruits of this earlier, thwarted experiment, and the women began from there. The two formed a dynamic partnership that lasted almost half a century—the Montessorian Gobbi bringing her expansive experience with young children; the theologian Cavalletti bringing her vast knowledge of the faith; both sharing a profound vision of the religious potential of the children in their midst.

In Cavalletti's home near the Piazza Navona, the women began what Montessori had first called an *atrium*. In the ancient Church, the atrium was the gathering place between the liturgical space of the Church and the street. It was the space in which the faithful recollected themselves before entering into the liturgy. It was also the place where the catechumens received instruction in the faith, in preparation for their full immersion within the Christian community. Cavalletti and Gobbi understood their atrium to serve a similar purpose; it was not to be a "children's Church" separate from the "adult Church," but rather an aid to the fuller participation of children in the liturgical and communal life of the one Church that includes the baptized of every age.

Over many years, Cavalletti and Gobbi developed numerous materials for the children to work with in the atrium. These included small models of the various objects children would see in their churches, dioramas and figures to accompany the reading of scripture, prayer cards, maps of the land of Israel, timelines of the history of salvation, and resources for further study of scripture and liturgy. When introducing a material to the children, the women would always listen to the children's responses and observe how they used the material. Materials that did not provoke intense reflection or individual work by the children were discarded. As in the Montessori environment, the children were understood to possess an "Inner Teacher"—now more explicitly recognized as the Holy Spirit—who would direct them toward that which was most essential in their own growing relationship with the divine. The adult was an observer, a matchmaker between God and the child, a co-listener and co-wonderer before the mystery of God, but the child was to lead the way. Through the children's consistent attraction to certain materials and their verbal and artistic reflections on their work with these materials, Cavalletti began to discern a unique tenor to the children's understanding of the Christian message—particular themes which captured their attention more than others and ways of expressing these themes that were unique to this age group. Slowly, a more stable collection of materials and reflections on these materials began to emerge.

Cavalletti began to share her growing insights through conference presentations and publications, always inviting others to listen deeply to the children around them and see what insights they would glean. Her 1961 text, *Teaching Doctrine and Liturgy,* represents an early stage of her theological reflection upon the work in which she and Gobbi were engaged. It was through *The Religious Potential of the Child,* however, that her observations became widespread. First published in Italian in 1979, the book was soon translated into English and Spanish.

By this time, her invitation to listen to and with children in a new way had been accepted by a number of other catechists. Atria began to spring up around Italy, elsewhere in Europe, Latin America, and the United States. Among the many impressed by the work of Cavalletti and her fellow catechists was a Mexican bishop who intuited that what he was observing in multiple, small, isolated settings was the beginning of a true international movement. It was he who first gave the effort a name—*Catechesis of the Good Shepherd*—based on the distinctive image of Christ to which the young children had been most drawn.

The bishop's intuitions quickly came to pass as cate-chists began to form loose associations with each other to share stories of their experiences with the children and sup-port each other in the work. In 1984, a small group of cate-chists in the United States, representing only about seven atria in all, united to form a national association of Catechists of the Good Shepherd. Since its origins, the number of atria registered with the national association in this country has grown exponentially to 658 at the printing of this book— a clear sign of the movement's appeal across the Atlantic divide. While remaining a Roman Catholic association, the method has been enthusiastically adopted by Episcopalian, Byzantine Catholic, Lutheran, Presbyterian, and Methodist congregations—a clear sign of the movement's appeal across the denominational divide. And, in the last ten years, the Catechesis has begun to grow in several new countries as well: Haiti, Uganda, Australia, South Africa, Korea, and Croatia, among others—a sign of the movement's continued appeal across cultures. It is also an indicator of a growing base of information about the theological reflection of chil-dren. For, in each of these atria around the globe, adults have been sitting beside children listening to the Word of God, gathering the observations, insights, and artwork of children concerning the Christian message. In the next chapter, we turn our attention to what it is that catechists of the Good Shepherd have discovered.

THE CHILD
AS THEOLOGIAN

In the introduction of this book, we defined theology according to the classic definition of Anselm of Canterbury: Theology is the work of faith seeking understanding. When we begin to look at a particular theology—in essence, a particular expression of faith seeking understanding—we need to ask two questions: Who are the people of faith doing this theology? And, what are the questions that are driving them to seek further understanding?

Initially, the first question may not seem to be especially important. What does it matter who is doing the theology? God is always the same God, right? Our experience since the Second Vatican Council, however, has taught us that it is enormously important. As suggested in chapter one, we have come to recognize that all works of theology are deeply influenced by the experience, culture, gender, and even developmental stage of their authors. It is helpful to note at the outset what factors are shaping a theology and to be aware of their impact.

When we speak about children's theological reflections, there are nine characteristics common to early childhood that catechists of the Good Shepherd have observed most influence the way in which children hear and interpret the Gospel. This doesn't mean that these traits belong exclusively to young children. Rather, they are human traits that are in some way true of each one of us no matter how old we are, but they are traits that are particularly dominant during early childhood. Let us look at these characteristics one by one:

- **Children are small.** It seems too obvious even to point out, doesn't it? There is, however, perhaps no more influential reality in the life of a child. Children are small creatures in an adult-sized world. Everyone and everything around them is much bigger and more powerful than they are. And yet, they recognize that there is a great power and energy inside of tiny things. They know it in their own bodies. What appears weak may be deceivingly strong. When children study the scripture, they read it through the lens of small-ness and weakness—drawn to those characters and events that seem too humble for God to work through, but, time and time again, are the locus for God's most powerful activity. They identify God's preference for the small as a thread that runs all the way through-out and unites the many books of the Bible.

- **Children are drawn toward what is most essential.** Children are not interested in the peripheral or the superfluous. They want to go straight to the heart of the matter. They want the greatest truths in the fewest words possible. Cavalletti notes that when children's magnet-like attraction to the essential is honored, they can help the Church to remember and treasure that which is most important in the faith. Children desire "rich food, and not too much of it," she stresses.[2]

- **Children want to be oriented to reality.** One of the
  most essential tasks of children is to figure out how
  the world they live in ticks, so that they are able to
  survive and make sense out of life. Hence, more than
  fantasy, children are deeply attracted toward what
  is real. Exposure to religion plays an important part of
  this orientation to reality because, at its core, religion
  is about that which is *most* real—the foundations
  upon which all of creation exists.

- **Children are filled with awe and wonder.** When
  children encounter the real world in action, they can
  become engrossed for long periods of time. If you
  have ever witnessed a child's fascination with a bug
  crawling across a leaf or a tiny bird egg that has
  fallen from its nest, you know the degree of concentra-
  tion of which children are capable and the kind of
  intense questioning such encounters provoke. Through
  experiences of awe and wonder, children are drawn into
  relationship with the Creator of all that is real. It has
  often been noted by catechists of the Good Shepherd
  that the natural first prayer of young children is
  praise and thanksgiving, and only later petition. The
  earliest religious experiences of children seem to be
  sparked by awe rather than need.

- **Children are attracted toward the beautiful.** One
  of the aspects of the real world that most inspires awe
  and wonder in a child is beauty. They take great delight
  in that which is solemn and simple, but attractive.
  This applies to environments and objects, but also
  to language. Children are drawn toward beautiful words
  and music, often copying the words meticulously

even when they can barely write, and then singing or proclaiming them with the deepest reverence. They are disturbed when others do not greet beauty with reverence. "I sang 'O Come, O Come Emmanuel' at the grocery store this week," stated one five-year-old. "But the other people didn't really understand."

- **Children are filled with joy.**   When children encounter what is beautiful, awesome, and essential, they express unreserved joy. Cavalletti notes that just as increased height and weight are signs that the child's physical needs have been met, joy is the sign that a child's spiritual needs are being met. The joy manifests itself not as a giddy frenzy, but rather a peaceful relaxation of the body, and often a contented sigh. For children, this kind of joy is the first and most important response to God's gifts. One five-year-old, when naming the sheep of the Good Shepherd, decided that they would be called "Hap," "Py," "Joy," and "Ful."

- **Children have a deep desire and capacity to be in loving relationship.**   Relationship—children teach us—is the most essential, the most beautiful, and the most real thing in the universe. It is their deepest need and, when it is met, it is their greatest joy. Because their capacity for relationship is so large, it can be difficult to satiate. The children's great hunger to love and be loved offers perhaps the best testimony we have to the foundational principle of Christian anthropology that humans are ultimately "wired" to be in relationship with God. For, only in God, does the child's need and capacity fully meet its match.

- **Children possess absorbent minds.**   The phrase
  absorbent mind, coined earlier by Montessori, refers
  to the way in which very young children receive
  and integrate the natural world, culture, language, and
  even religious practice. Before developing skills for
  reasoning and logic, children learn through a process
  similar to osmosis: without the ability to filter, they
  unconsciously absorb their environment. If children
  possess an Inner Teacher who directs them toward
  what they need to grow, the environment is the Outer
  Teacher that can either help meet those needs or
  stifle them. Children's theology highlights the importance of sacred space and of all other environments
  in the religious formation of a community.

- **Children learn best through the repetitive work of
  their hands.**   Though children absorb through all of
  their senses, learning that is absorbed through the hand
  is especially effective. For a child, to do or to touch
  is far more impressive than only to hear or to see. Young
  children are not particularly interested in the end
  product of their work, but in the doing itself, over and
  over again. When this trait is applied to the study of
  theology, children reflect on the truths of the faith in a
  circular, rather than linear, fashion. Like the liturgical
  calendar, they will return again and again to the
  themes they find essential and continually draw new
  connections between these themes—generally while
  in the process of working with a familiar material
  or through artwork.

These nine characteristics permeate the theology that children express and give dit its unique flavor. They shape the

way in which children hear, meditate upon, and respond to questions of faith. But now, let us turn to the questions themselves. What are those core queries, arising from the life experiences of small children that compel their theological journey? Cavalletti categorizes the many questions she has heard children ask in the atrium into three main areas:

- **The Mystery of Relationship**   The very first set of questions children express have to do with the mystery of relationship: Who really are you, Lord? Who am I, in light of that? How do I come to know you? What is the nature of our relationship? When did our relationship begin? How can our relationship grow deeper? How can we celebrate our relationship?

- **The Mystery of Life and Death**   While still very young, children also begin to ask questions relating to the mystery of life and death: Where was I before I was born? How did I get here? Where is my grandmother who has died? Will I die? What will happen after I die? What is life? What is death?

- **The Mystery of Time**   A third set of questions, prevalent more among older children, ponders the mystery of time: What is time? Does it have a beginning? Is time moving forward or is it cyclical? Will it go on forever or will it have an end? Where does my time fall in the history of time? What is my role in this history to be?

Children bring these questions to intersect with a broad and deep Christian tradition. In the atrium, they sift through the scriptures and contemporary liturgical practice of the

Church to identify those images—in word, sign, story, and gesture—that best enable them to engage the depth of these three mysteries. In the following chapters, we will look at several images from the heart of our faith tradition that children have identified as being particularly helpful in their own attempt to find meaning. We will also look at the connections they make between these images, offering us a new way of synthesizing our faith tradition.

The Mystery of Relationship

In the opening of his *Confessions,* Augustine of Hippo states, "Our hearts are restless, until they rest in You, O Lord."[3] The saint's conviction could be considered the cornerstone of children's theology—the first building block upon which all else depends. God and humanity were meant for one another, children believe. If we want to understand what is true and real and essential, they say, we must first understand the nature of this relationship.

THE MINGLING OF THE WATER AND THE WINE
Children respond with reverent joy to many different images from the Christian tradition that illumine for them the nature of the relationship between God and humanity. One of the earliest images to which they are deeply attracted is the gesture of the mingling of the water and the wine in the chalice. In the atrium, the children repeatedly prepare two cruets— one with wine, the other with water—as they would see in the celebration of Eucharist. Into a clear wine glass, they pour all of the wine and just a few drops of the water while pondering a clue given by the early Church: the wine represents divinity (God); the water represents humanity (us). They wonder about what happens to the water. They wonder whether the water and wine can be separated again.

Out of their meditation on the experience, the children tell us that, in comparison to God, humanity is quite tiny. But, when humanity and divinity meet, an amazing thing happens: humanity loses itself in awe and is absorbed by the other. In children's theology, there is nothing inherently incompatible between humanity and divinity. They are meant for one another and mingle freely. "The gesture," said one child, "tells us that God and us—we are very close." "Nothing can separate us again," said another. Jesus, in the children's understanding, is evidence of our compatibility. In Jesus, the human's great desire to be in relationship with God and God's great desire to be in relationship with us met in a single person. Jesus is the full and complete mingling of the water and the wine.

Each of us, however, is invited to enjoy this intimate union with God. In the gesture of the mingling of water and wine, children recognize a personal invitation to lose themselves by falling in love with God. "When does this happen?" one six-year-old asked the catechist and another child as they gathered near the work. "I wonder," the catechist replied, "What do you think?" "In heaven," the six-year-old stated. "But God is everywhere," said the other child. Later, the six-year-old approached the catechist. "I have been thinking," he said, "if God is everywhere, then what happens in the cup could happen right here today." Sometimes it does.

THE GOOD SHEPHERD

In our tradition, there are many images of God that have captured the human imagination and affection. For young children, the image that most readily effects a deep "falling in love" with the divine is the image of the Good Shepherd found in the Gospel of John. The atrium material related to this parable—a simple circular sheepfold with a wooden shepherd figure and several wooden sheep—is one of the oldest and most beloved in the Catechesis. Although first introduced at the tender age of three, the children return to it over and over again as they grow and consistently relate new materials and presentations back to this earlier work. The image of the Good Shepherd seems to encapsulate for the child what is most desirable and essential in a relationship: the joy of being known by name, of having a home, of being loved unconditionally, of having someone to love without fear of rejection, of having all of one's needs tended to. While the totality of the Shepherd's gift of self is very present in the Johannine parable, the children emphasize that the gift of the Shepherd's life was not a one-time event, but a way of living. Before the Good Shepherd died for his sheep, he lived every moment of his life for them. Every action was done, every word spoken, and every decision made with them in mind.

The children's awareness that they are sheep of the Good Shepherd often dawns slowly. Sometimes it happens through artwork: a child will be drawing the Good Shepherd and the sheep and suddenly switch over to drawing people. Sometimes it happens in the midst of working with the material: a child will begin to line the sheep up behind the Shepherd in a "boy's line" and a "girl's line" and give them the names of classmates from school. And, sometimes, a child stands and makes the proclamation clearly and with great dignity: "One of the sheep is named Joseph," five-year-old Joseph spontaneously proclaimed. In children's theological reflections, the process of coming to an awareness of one's status as a sheep of the Good Shepherd is an essential stage of the Christian journey. In contrast to more evangelical theologies, the pivotal moment in one's faith life is not so much recognizing and choosing Jesus as one's "personal

Lord and Savior" as it is recognizing oneself as someone who has been personally chosen. Children regard those who live without this knowledge as truly deprived. In the wake of the September 11, 2001 events, while pondering how persons could have chosen such hurtful actions, the four- to six-year-olds in our parish atrium decided, "They did not know that they were sheep of the Good Shepherd."

The mission of the Good Shepherd, stated in John 10:10, summarizes perhaps better than any other scripture passage the heart of children's theology: "I have come that they may have life, and have it in abundance." The God that children know and proclaim is the God of life. This God is the source of life. This God loves life and embraces life, like the children do. And, this God wants to give life freely and abundantly. There is no scarcity or stinginess in the God of children. There is no fear that God's life will run out, or that if one person receives it someone else will obtain less. God's life is great. There is plenty for all.

THE EUCHARIST

Like every loving relationship, relationship with God calls for moments of celebration. In children's theology, the sacraments, particularly the sacrament of Eucharist, are understood to be such moments. Sacrament, they believe, is a mediated encounter between God and humanity that emerges out of and celebrates their great desire to be with one another. The reflection of one group of four- to six-year-olds in the atrium over the course of the Easter season captures the spirit of their understanding well: When meditating on the parable of the Good Shepherd, this group of children repeatedly lifted up Jesus' love for his sheep and his desire to be with them always. First he lived his whole life for them, they said. He loved them so much that he was willing to die for them.

But, after reading the scripture passage of the empty tomb from Luke, one of the four-year-olds added, "He loved them so much, he could not stay dead. He had to rise, so that he could always be with them." The other children agreed: not only did Jesus live and die for them, he rose for them. Later in the season, they made a further connection to the sacramental life: the risen Jesus, ascended to heaven, can no longer be seen by his sheep, but out of love for them and desire to be with them always, offers the gift of Eucharist so that he might remain present with them in a most particular way until that day when they can see him face to face. The Good Shepherd is always with his sheep, the children asserted, but we celebrate that presence in a special way through the bread and the wine.

In Eucharist, children perceive that the whole flock gathers around the Good Shepherd—each sheep called individually by name to be there, but called to come together, and through Eucharist, to be united even more closely to one another. In the fascinating drawing of one five-year-old boy, the circular torso of the Good Shepherd has become the altar table, with the bread and the wine in the center over the heart. The head is that of the Good Shepherd, with a sheep hoisted around his neck. The appendages of his body, however, have become people—truly an image of the Body of Christ. Sometimes the children intuit a gathering even larger than the one they can see in their own communities. "Every Sunday, in churches all over the country," asserted one six-year-old, "the Good Shepherd is calling his sheep to gather around him at their altar tables so he can be with them." "All over the world," corrected another. "All over the universe," shouted a third with her arms outstretched.

BAPTISM

But how is it that we have come to celebrate around this table? How is it that we first entered into this profound relationship with both the Shepherd and the others in his sheepfold? Children experience immense pride and joy in knowing that there was a particular moment in which they were first called by name, welcomed into the fold, and set on a path toward the table—the moment of Baptism. "I have been baptized," one three-year-old proclaimed, standing on the pew as the priest and acolyte processed down the aisle at the beginning of Eucharist. As keen interpreters of symbol, their theology of Baptism is primarily derived from the meaning they attribute to the sacramental signs associated with the baptismal rite: the light, the white garment, the water, the Word, the oils, and the sign of the cross.

In contrast to most adults, the first attractive and meaningful sign of Baptism for the youngest child is not water, but light. Light is interpreted by children to mean joy, safety, freedom from fear, understanding, and beauty. The lit candle is a magnet to their eyes and quickly stills their bodies. Very early on, children begin to associate light with God. One child, age four, arrived at the atrium one morning with the announcement: "God told me I would meet him here today." "Did he tell you where?" the assistant asked. "No," the child replied. Later in the session, however, when she lit a small candle, the boy's eyes grew wide. "There God is!" he exclaimed and sat for a long time in quiet conversation.

The association of God with light is so evocative for the child that we could identify it as the second most favored image for the divine in their doing of theology. The children are particularly drawn to scripture passages that speak of Christ as being Light—from the prophecy of Isaiah to the star over Bethlehem; from the eclipse of the sun at his death to his rising on the dawn of the third day. Christ is "the light of the world," the children profess with John 8:12; a light stronger than the darkness of death, they affirm with the liturgy of the Easter Vigil. And, they are truly enchanted with the baptismal image of the individual taper lit from the Paschal candle: a sharing in the inextinguishable Light of the risen Christ.

The children often draw parallels or merge the image of baptismal light with that of the Good Shepherd and the sheepfold. In their artwork, children have often drawn the sheep as yellow ("full of light") or holding candles. In a drawing by another five-year-old Italian boy, a number of small, individually lit tapers surround a large Paschal candle inside of a circle, much like the sheep surround the Good Shepherd in the fold. Baptism, the children tell us, is an intimate sharing in the light and life of the Good Shepherd. Through this sacrament, we enter into a community of light. The white garment is a further extension of the image for them—a sign that we are covered in light, both interiorly and exteriorly.

The water of Baptism is also very alluring, but for the youngest of children, it does not primarily connote the washing away of sin in the same way that it might in an adult theology of Baptism. Rather, water, like light, is beautiful, refreshing, and magnetic in its attraction. It evokes memories of happiness and comfort. It quenches thirst. Though too much of it can be dangerous, children recognize that all things need it to grow and thrive. Likewise, the oils are soothing. They feel good to touch. They are beautiful to look at. The oil of chrism, in particular, smells wonderful, too.

Baptism, the children infer, is about receiving all that is most beautiful and essential in life. It is about being gifted with what we most need to live—not in scant proportions, but in abundance. They want to know that they have received not a sprinkling of water, but an immersion in the pool; not a drop of oil, but a lavish outpouring. "How did it feel when you went into the water?" one five-year-old consistently quizzed an assistant who was baptized as an adult at the Easter Vigil. "How did the oil feel? How did it feel to receive the light?" For children, who experience so much through their senses, Baptism is a feast of sight and smell and touch.

The baptismal signing with the cross, in children's theology, is often understood to be a sort of branding by which the Good Shepherd permanently marks a sheep as belonging to his fold and his fold only. In their artwork, children will often draw sheep and people with crosses on their foreheads. The closing cross of blessing, made over the parents and the community, is understood to be like the shield of the Good Shepherd who always goes before his sheep, protecting them and clearing the way. While there are occasional hints of a Paschal overtone in their understanding of the cross, they primarily identify it simply as Jesus' sign, the sign that signifies the special relationship they have with him.

LIFE IN THE TRUE VINE

Baptism, in the theology of children, is never an end in itself, but the beginning of a life-long, joy-filled relationship. It is an abundant gifting with all that will be needed for the relationship to continue and flourish. As children grow older, their awareness of what it means to live a baptized life continues to evolve, and they begin to seek images that will express even more fully the degree of intimacy to which they feel invited in the sacraments. When the children are around the age of six, the catechists begin to lift up a third Johannine icon—in addition to the Good Shepherd and Light—that helps the children to further penetrate the true nature of their relationship with the divine and with each other. This is the image of the True Vine from John 15.

In contrast to the parable of the Good Shepherd that uses the language of *calling* and *following,* the parable of the True Vine repeatedly uses the verb *remain*—suggesting a pre-existing relationship that invites not movement but faithfulness, not breadth but depth. The image of relationship in the parable of the True Vine is perhaps even more intimate than that of the Good Shepherd and the sheep. Now, the disciples are branches of Christ's "Vine," a plant that does not exist separate from its branches. In Baptism, the children say, we become a shoot on the True Vine—a shoot which, if continually nourished by the sap that first caused it to bud, will grow into a larger branch and bear fruit. They recognize that this sap by which they live and grow is the same sap that nourishes the whole vine—the sap of the Spirit of the risen Christ. The growth and fruitfulness of the vine give great joy to God the Father, the Vine-tender, and increase God's glory. The parable becomes for them an image of the abundant relational life of the Trinity in which they are invited to participate.

Death is not an obstacle to life in the True Vine, children believe. Since the sap is the Spirit of the risen Christ, the vine is stronger than death and can cross and recross the boundaries of space and time. The only things that can cause decay in the vine are obstacles that we create to slow or halt the flow of sap—in essence, sin.

For children, sin is not the natural proclivity of the human beings who have the Spirit-sap of the risen Christ coursing through their veins. The natural proclivity of those who dwell in the vine is love. When you are in a loving relationship you want to do right by those that you love. Good actions blossom forth organically like fruit from the vine. Rather, it is sin that is the peculiarity. Sin is a sign that the relationship is not what it should be, not what it could be. Sin is a tragedy. It impedes the sap from freely reaching all of the branches of the vine—our own branch—but also the branches that are linked to ours. In blocking the sap, sin decreases the fruitfulness of the vine, lessening the Father's glory. But, most sadly perhaps, in the view of the child, sin hinders the joy of relationship. Life in the vine, children proclaim with the Johannine Jesus, is supposed to be all about joy: "All this I tell you that my joy may be yours and your joy may be complete" (John 15:11).

The Mystery of Life and Death

Earlier, in chapter three, we noted that one of the traits of young children that most influences their theology is a desire to be oriented toward reality. Young children want to make sense of the day-to-day world around them and to learn how to function harmoniously in it. To some degree, culture serves this purpose. Culture is the environment in which each of us lives twenty-four hours a day. It passes on to us habits of thought and a sense of what is normal. It gives us the language in which we communicate with others. It offers us a communal lens through which we can interpret everyday interactions. The child's desire to be oriented to reality, however, is not satiated by culture's responses. Children need to go far deeper; they want to peek under the floorboards of culture's house and discover the foundations upon which their daily existence rests, the foundations upon which the existence of the universe rests. They wish to determine not only how to survive in life, but even more essential: What *is* life? What is it that makes life possible?

THE KINGDOM OF GOD

Children find help for their quest in Jesus' teaching about the kingdom of God. Proclaiming and heralding the kingdom lies at the heart of Jesus' mission. When Jesus wanted to talk about what was most essential, he spoke about the kingdom of God. When he wanted to peel back the floorboards to orient his listeners to the deepest reality in the universe, Jesus preached the kingdom. The kingdom is a truth too great to be contained in discursive speech. "He spoke to them in parables only," reads the Gospel of Matthew, "to fulfill what had been said through the prophet: 'I will open my mouth in parables, I will announce what has lain hidden since the foundation of the world' " (Matthew 13:34b–35).

The very first images of the kingdom to which the children are drawn come from the verses surrounding this intriguing Matthean verse: the mustard seed, the precious pearl, the hidden treasure, and the leaven. In these parables the children have repeatedly chosen, two dominant themes emerge. First, the kingdom of God is a thing of great preciousness and beauty, more valuable than any other possession. Second, the kingdom has something to do with the mystery of growth and transformation, a mysterious energy moving within the small and hidden leading it to ever more abundant life.

This latter insight resonates deeply with the children's own experience of life. As we noted earlier, children know what it means to be small and hidden while possessing an incredible energy and potential inside. In the proclamation of the kingdom, they recognize immediately that God is the source of this energy. When things grow and change, they say, it is God's own power that is at work—a sign of God's reigning. They delight to hear that smallness is no obstacle for God—that it is, in fact, God's preferred location to initiate something wonderful.

Children see the principle of the kingdom of God alive in all of creation. It is not only mustard seeds or leaven or their own bodies that begin in obscurity, grow, and change.

Rather, this same mysterious energy is at work in every blade of grass, in every tree and flower, in every animal, even in the universe itself—which, in the best guess of contemporary science, began as something smaller even than a single atom, smaller than a mustard seed. "It is the secret of creation," writes Cavalletti. She says, ". . . That vital breath which swells the small mustard seed and makes it become a great tree is the breath within all that is created, and it calls [humanity] forth into a marvelous movement that goes, incredibly, from the less to the more."[4]

The kingdom of God was alive in a most particular way, they realize, in the person of Jesus, who lived what he preached. "Jesus was like the yeast," one eight-year-old who regularly made leavened dough in the atrium spontaneously stated. "His rising from the dead changed everything." At another time, shortly after Christmas, a six-year-old blurted out, "Jesus was like a mustard seed." "How?" the catechist asked. "Because he started very, very small in a stable in Bethlehem and grew to be great." Jesus, for the child, is the example par excellence of what life looks like when it is animated by the power of God. His life mirrors the fundamental progression of the universe from a "less to a more."

THE GRAIN OF WHEAT
The realization that there exists a thrust from "less to more" animating the universe raises a question, however: What is the role of death in this kingdom? Is it opposed to the kingdom? Is it a part of the kingdom? Our Christian tradition has offered a range of approaches to this question. For children, Jesus' observations about the grain of wheat in John 12:24 have served as a particularly rich source of meditation on the mystery of life and death. They recognize in his words a further insight into their earlier reflection on the mustard seed:

seeds possess within themselves an amazing energy and power, but in order for this energy and power to be unleashed, the seed must be buried beneath the soil. Although hidden from the eye, change is taking place and new life is emerging while the seed decays.

Cavalletti describes the response of one child (age 4½) in her writing: After examining wheat seeds at various stages of growth and transformation, the child drew a flower. "The catechist asked her, 'Where is the seed?' and Cecelia answered, 'You can't see it because it's dead. It has given its life to the plant.' After a pause, she continued, 'Without the seed the plant can't grow. The seed isn't dead, though; it's just that its life has gone into the stem and the roots.' "[5] At another time, an eight-year-old girl, reflecting on the same verse, marveled at the many grains on a stalk of wheat that had grown from just one seed. She counted them until she reached 80. "Jesus said his own death was like this?" she asked. "Yes," the catechist replied. "Then what are the many grains that have grown from his seed?" She paused for just a brief moment before answering her own question: "Oh, I see now. It is us—the Church." Later she added, "Someday each of us will have to lay down our lives if the life in Jesus' seed is going to keep growing."

Death, in children's theology, is not opposed to God's work in the universe. Rather, God works through it to bring the "lesser" to the "more." Cavalletti summarizes,

> This, it seems to us, is the fundamental law of life,
> as incredible as it may seem: Life develops through
> a series of successive "deaths," which lead us to
> live always more fully, because in each death there is
> the seed of the resurrection. The secret of reality seems
> to be that it always preserves in itself the seed of the

resurrection, and the more the seed is reduced and hidden, the more powerful it becomes. What we call death is the diminishing of the force of life to its most imperceptible expression; but it is from the most tenuous forms of life that—paradoxically—life blossoms ever richer.[6]

LIVING IN HARMONY WITH THE KINGDOM

The announcement of the kingdom of God confirms the children's deepest intuitions and greatest hopes about what—or rather, "who"—it is that undergirds all life, and how this "who" operates. They recognize that God has structured the universe in such a way that it enables a burgeoning of life. As the children grow older, they grow increasingly interested in observing this structure at work, understanding it, and living in harmony with it. The sun rises and sets with regularity, they note. Seasons come and go with some predictability. The stars are in the same patterns each night. In their studies, they discover some animals eat other animals and the ecosystem is able to stay in balance. They learn that scientists can tell exactly when the tide will rise and fall and which night of the month the moon will be full and which night it will disappear entirely. Children discern an unwritten set of laws, which all of nature seems to obey without resistance—laws that make it possible for life to go on and, moreover, to flourish. The laws are so intricate and complex that no human has yet discovered their every nuance, much less been able to replicate them. But, such laws exist. They are the superstructure of God's kingdom.

For children, the natural order of the created world provides a framework for reflection on human response to the kingdom of God. If all of creation lives in harmony according to divinely inspired laws, then, they reckon, humans must be invited to participate in the harmony by acquiescence to law as well. The children identify the maxims of the Gospels, particularly from the Sermon on the Mount, as the human parallel to nature's law. These laws are given as guides to humanity so that we can assume the role we have been created to play in the universe and enjoy the abundant life that God desires for all of creation.

The difference, the children highlight, is that humans have the potential to choose to obey the maxims and move with the current that undergirds the universe or not. The only other being who has this ability to choose is God. For children, this indicates that humanity has a very special role within the kingdom. Like God, humanity possesses intelligence that is to be motivated only by love, only by the desire for the flourishing of life. This unique expectation is summarized in the words of the young lawyer to Jesus: "You shall love the Lord your God with all your heart, with all your soul, with all your strength, and with all your mind; and your neighbor as yourself" (Luke 10:27). The most fundamental law for humanity is to love. The other maxims only serve to underscore and illumine this command. When we love, we not only enjoy relationship with God and each other, we also fulfill a cosmic law that puts us in harmony with all of creation. When we embrace this law and collaborate with the energy and power of the kingdom, we enjoy the abundant life God desires for us. When we struggle against it, the whole universe experiences disharmony.

THE MYSTERY OF TIME

Children love deeply the images the Gospels offer of the kingdom of God and revel in what these images unlock for them. As they continue to sit with these images, however, they begin to bring new questions to the conversation. They want to know not only *what* the kingdom of God is like, but also *when* it began and *where* it is heading. Did the kingdom start with Jesus, or does the kingdom have a longer history? Will the kingdom always look as it does now, or are we progressing somewhere? Will the kingdom have an end? If so, when will this be? When children ask these questions, they have begun to wrestle with the mystery of time.

For children before the age of six, there is little awareness of time. All of the past is conceived in terms of "yesterdays" and all of the future is contained in "tomorrow." They have little vocabulary that can capture greater expanses of time. For children over the age of six, however, time becomes a central theological theme. It is part of the reality in which they find themselves immersed and to which they desire to be oriented. They come to realize that time has gone on much longer than they previously had been able to imagine and that the future may extend beyond the horizon of their vision. Amidst such dizzying immensity, they need to know where their age and culture fit into the bigger picture and what the purpose of their particular lives is in this history. They discover that while space is a fixed reality that can be dominated and mastered, time is not. Time eludes every attempt to take hold of it. It cannot be stopped or manipulated. Time belongs exclusively to God and, hence, has an inherently spiritual element to it.

THE JEWISH UNDERSTANDING OF HISTORY

Within the Jewish tradition that forms the foundation for Christianity, children identify a distinctive perspective on time that is not paralleled in other cultures of biblical times. The Jews perceived time as moving forward, despite the cyclical rhythm of nature in which time seemed only to repeat itself. Moreover, it moved forward with a purpose, according to a larger plan designed and actively tended by God. The discernment of the plan, however, was often challenging. Sometimes it was difficult to detect the *modus operandi* of God. Understanding the plan of God required a deep listening, an acute attentiveness to the marvelous deeds of God in the history of the Jewish people, and a committed seeking for patterns in these vast actions accomplished by God in the experience of the Jewish people.

In the Jewish struggle to listen and discern, children find a model for their own task. Just as the children interpret faith through the lens of their physical smallness in a large world, the Jewish people interpreted history through the lens of their own smallness as an insignificant, originally nomadic, nation in the midst of great civilizations. Like the children, the Jewish people discern that God has called them by name, despite—and maybe, because of—their smallness. They discern that God has chosen to do great things in them, to reveal God's reign to the world because God has consistently chosen the lowly and the marginalized and the hidden to be collaborators in bringing God's plan to fruition. Sometimes this insight is obscured, even within the pages of scripture, but it can be traced throughout the biblical literature, Cavalletti states, like a " 'golden thread' that binds together the history that God is creating in collaboration with human kind."[7]

ON A GLOBAL SCALE

In their doing of theology, children take the Jewish framework of history as time moving forward guided by a divine hand and integrate it with the evolutionary approach to history to which they are commonly exposed in their education. They do not perceive the expansiveness of time central to the evolutionary approach as contrary to biblical faith, but rather as further evidence of the tremendous care and patience with which God prepares for each new moment in God's plan. Having already fallen in love with the tender, relational God illuminated by Jesus the Good Shepherd, they interpret the magnificent beauty and diversity of creation as a further indication of this God's love for them. They marvel at the mineral world with its incredible variety of rocks and metals: the marble and iron so useful in building, the salt that seasons and preserves food, the diamonds and rubies found in jewelry, the precious metals used for commerce, the flint that sparks a fire. They delight in the abundance of the plant world: the medicinal herbs, the mighty trees that shade the land and provide wood for homes, the beautiful and aromatic flowers, the bountiful array of vegetables and fruits, the cotton and flax that are woven into clothing. They glory in the wealth of the animal world: from the tiniest one-celled organisms to the great elephant, the colorful fish of the sea, the melodic birds of the air, donkeys that aid in carrying burdens, sheep that share their wool, cows and pigs that provide meat, companion dogs and cats.

Children recognize that humans arrived on this scene like guests at a banquet—discovering that everything they needed, but even more than that, everything they could ever *want,* had already been prepared in advance. In their anthropology, what distinguishes humanity from the remainder of creation is the ability to step back and wonder, Who has made all of this for me? This capacity to wonder, they note, evokes the capacity to be thankful, and the capacity—for the first time in all of the millennia upon millennia of evolving creation—to love the Creator in return. As noted in earlier chapters, humans are distinguished from other mammals, first and foremost, by their capacity to love.

The children, however, recognize a second distinguishing characteristic among human beings, also suggested earlier—the capacity to transform the earth through the work of the hand, guided by intelligence. While the entire natural world contributes unconsciously in its own way to the fulfillment of God's plan, humans have a uniquely conscious role in the transformation of creation, collaborating with God to bring it toward an ever-greater "fullness of life." The tiny algae are transformed into penicillin. Emeralds may be cut and polished to be enjoyed as gems. The wheat of the field is converted into bread. Humans are of creation and yet set above creation, to help bring it to its fuller potential.

And, yet, this reality raises a question in the mind of the child: By the work of whose hands would humanity be transformed and reach its fuller potential? Like Anselm, in his classic text, *Why the God-Man?,* children say that it would have to be one like us and yet set above us. Despite the many, many gifts that God prepared through the work of creation, the children discern that there was an even greater gift that God wanted to give: the gift of God's very own self, God's very own life—*the* fullness of life. It makes sense to the children that this gift was a long time in coming. It took much preparation—the formation of a people, wooed by miraculous events, shaped by law, purified by prophets, enlightened by sages—in which gradually the Light and Life of God became ever more present to humanity, culminating in the Light and Life of Jesus Christ. In the Light and Life of Christ, children say, a new moment dawned in the history of time. By the work of Jesus' hands, the blind were made to see, the lame were made to walk, the lonely were held, the outcasts were included. And, by the work of Jesus' hands—bound and nailed to the cross in the fullness of love, resurrected from the grave while still bearing the wounds—humanity itself was transformed. We were able to see humanity's fullest potential.

The Resurrection of Christ gives evidence of where God's plan is heading. One day, the "fullness of life" experienced by Jesus will be experienced by all of creation. Our scriptures speak of this day as the *parousia*. Though we have many descriptions of it, the children express greatest delight in the image offered in 1 Corinthians 15:28: the day when God will be "all in all." Given the expanse of past history, the children often think that the *parousia* might take a long time. They acknowledge that in the two thousand years since Jesus, the Light and Life of his risen Spirit have touched many across the globe, but not all, and that those who have been touched are themselves transformed only slowly and with time. They often pray, however, that it will come very quickly. "Make the *parousia* come fast!" exclaimed one eight-year-old around the prayer table. One could not help but think of the prayer of the earliest Christian communities: *"Maranatha!"*

It is important to note, however, that children are not generally discouraged by the delay of the *parousia*. They refer to the time between the present and the *parousia* as "the blank page"—that page of history that is yet to be written, even though the last one has already been written. As with all of the pages of history, they state that God is the author of this page, but they also know that God intends to write it through the work of human hands. Children will frequently speak of the necessity of opening and enjoying the gifts they have been given in the world of creation and through Baptism, and then using these gifts—transforming them by the work of their hands—to hasten the coming of the *parousia*. They desire to be collaborators in the fulfillment of God's Plan.

The Eucharistic meal, children tell us, manifests what is taking place in time. It lifts up for us in broad, essential strokes the dynamic that undergirds all of history, enabling us to see it more clearly. From the abundance of creation, humanity takes the grapes of the vine and the grains of wheat and transforms them into wine and bread through the work of its hands. Set upon the altar table, these humble gifts are transformed again through the power of God and infused with God's own presence. Like Jesus, they are creation in which God has become "all in all." They are a sign of what shall take place in all of creation at the *parousia* and, in partaking of the meal, we move closer to that promised day when God's plan to bring all of creation to a fullness of life shall reach its completion.

WHAT CHILDREN HAVE TO TEACH US ABOUT PREACHING

An Approach

We began this book with an intriguing, albeit unusual, question: What do children have to teach us about preaching? One possibility is to read this question very narrowly and consider what implications the presented material about children and children's theology has for preaching to children. However, if we hold fast to the original premise of chapter one—that children's theology is a gift for the whole Church—we will want to conceive of the question more broadly. Does the wisdom gleaned by catechists of the Good Shepherd about children, their questions, and their theology suggest anything for the ministry of preaching in general?

Karl Rahner, one of the only prominent theologians of the past century to develop a theology of childhood, claimed that, from the Christian perspective of the human person, the experience of childhood is not a stage that passes away and is replaced by adulthood. Rather, since each human being is an eternal being, childhood has an eternal nature. Rahner argued:

> We do not lose childhood as that which recedes ever
> further into our past, that which remains behind as
> we advance forward in time, but rather we go toward

it as that which has been achieved in time and redeemed forever in time. We only *become* the children whom we *were* because we gather up time—and in this our childhood too—into our eternity. Throughout our entire life span . . . childhood may always remain open. And we may still have to go on living through our own childhood in our life taken as a whole because it always remains an open question for us.[8]

My own experience as a catechist and adult educator has confirmed for me Rahner's key insight: at the core of every human person is a child—a child who is not lost to time. Hence, if we are looking to speak a word that can be heard across ages and ethnicities, if we are looking for what experience all human beings hold in common, our eternal childhood is clearly a common denominator of great potential. It turns out that, while we develop additional needs and capacities as we grow, we never lose the core needs and capacities of our childhood. The urge to touch and to do things repetitively with our own hands, the desire for what is essential, the joy we experience when we find it, the love of beauty—these things always remain with us. And the questions of childhood—what it means to be in relationship, the meaning of life and death, the mystery of time—these are not exhausted in youth. The questions of childhood remain always open. When our preaching wrestles with these questions, when it searches the Christian tradition for insight into these mysteries, when it lets people touch and revel in them, it produces a deep sigh of contentment not only in children, but in adults as well.

In the introduction of this book, we considered the difficulties of preaching in the contemporary world and acknowledged that in order to continue this ministry, preachers must possess a deep hope that God can and will do great things out of very small and humble messengers. We called it mustard seed preaching. In looking at the theology of children, as discerned by the Catechesis of the Good Shepherd, we can see that it is grounded in a similar hope and confidence—so much so that we might choose to call it mustard seed theology. In the closing chapters of this book, let us consider how mustard seed theology might be an aid to mustard seed preaching, giving it a set of guiding principles and themes consistent with its foundational hope. This chapter will lift up eight guiding principles. The next chapter will provide a look at the themes.

LISTEN WITH THE LITTLE

Mustard seed preachers share a special affinity with those who are small and marginalized and faced with seemingly impossible, immense tasks. As such, part of their spirituality will be to sit in solidarity with the "little ones" before the Word of God. They will assume a posture of listening together to the Word of God and will attempt to hear it from the perspective of their fellow listeners. Preachers will regularly set aside time in their schedules to be with those who are on the margins of society—be they poor, disabled, children, or those in nursing homes. For many, ministry among these populations may already constitute a major part of daily life. For others, it may require more deliberate planning. In any case, preachers are encouraged by the approach of mustard seed theology to be very intentional in encounters to listen as well as to speak, to receive as well as to offer, to humbly ask what the children hear and understand of scripture and life instead of only teaching what adults hear and understand.

One of the most unexpected blessings of the past year for me has been a practice that began quite spontaneously in our atrium one Sunday while gathered with three- to six-year-old children in prayer at the end of a session. After we had offered our prayers, I suggested that we close our eyes and open our ears to see if God had anything special to speak to our hearts today. After about thirty seconds, I invited them to share what they had heard, if they wanted to. "God says He loves me very much," one child volunteered. "He says I am precious," another stated. Each week, we have continued the practice of listening together, trying to extend the silence. The children have continued to share profound messages— often around the theme of their own identity as the beloved of God. As one whose heart is harder of hearing, it has been a gift to be close to hearts that do hear, and to be present as they utter these insights fresh from the divine encounter.

PREACH RESPECTFULLY

There is an adage among missionaries that admonishes recent arrivals to approach the new culture with reverence, for "God was here before we arrived." Mustard seed preachers recognize that the same wisdom applies to congregations. Like children, congregations are not blank slates. God has already been at work in the congregants' lives before the preacher arrives. The Inner Teacher has already been guiding their hearts toward what gives life. One catechist-priest from Massachusetts states:

> The most revolutionary element [of the Catechesis of the Good Shepherd] for me was the understanding that the child is already a spiritual being. By implication, this meant the adult is also already a spiritual being. So often in my preaching training, I think we thought

that we needed to create a spiritual being, but the
person is already spiritual. I don't need to put something divine into the person; the divine is already
in the human. As a preacher, I can help people connect
to it, liberate it. This has given me a different view of
the congregation I preach to.

This "different view" is reflected in the respectful style
of mustard seed preaching. Mustard seed preachers honor the
experience of God that congregations have had and accept
that it may be different from their own. The purpose of preaching is not to persuade congregants to adopt the preachers'
spiritual path, but to assist them in discovering and faithfully
walking the particular path God has paved for them. It
is about helping them to listen for the voice of the Inner
Teacher—the call of the Good Shepherd in their own lives.

PREACHING AS MATCHMAKING

If preaching is to assist people in following the Shepherd's
call, its first and primary aim is to aid a falling in love with
God. The vision of preaching that emerges from mustard
seed theology is distinctive in this regard. Whereas other
theologies might envision the primary aim of preaching as
explaining the scripture in everyday language, or challenging the congregation toward a conversion of life, mustard
seed theology conceives of preaching as "matchmaking." It
wants to help God and humanity—who are already wired for
relationship with each other—to make that connection. If listeners fall in love with God, everything else will follow. They
will want to learn more about God. They will want to do
right by their beloved and turn their lives around. But, now
these actions will be rooted in love. The approach of mustard seed theology challenges preachers to prepare by asking

the following questions: What in this scripture passage helps me to fall more deeply in love with God? How can I preach this passage in such a way that the assembled might fall more deeply in love with God? How can I help make the match?

One of the challenges when conceiving of the preacher as a matchmaker is that the preacher doesn't always get to go on the date. In the atrium, this phenomenon is sometimes referred to as the "poverty of the catechist." There are things that go on between God and the child that we are not privy to. There are sacred moments when we wish we could draw nearer to eavesdrop upon the child's whispers as they work. But, we must move out of the way and know that our particular service has been rendered. Preachers experience a similar poverty. Sometimes their words strike chords that they do not know have been touched. Most of the time they never know if their words have had any lasting effect. Sometimes preachers are tempted to chaperone every minute of the relationship, tidy up every loose end, neatly answer every question, and not allow any space for the relationship to flourish without oversight. Mustard seed preachers are invited to trust that God will pick up where they have left off and to actually create silences within prayer where relationship with God can flourish.

PREACHING AS ORIENTATION TOWARD REALITY

If aiding a falling-in-love is the primary aim of mustard seed preaching, orientation to reality is a close second. If Jesus' preaching continually sought to orient his listeners to the reality he perceived most central in the universe—the kingdom of God—then surely this must be equally important to preachers today. Congregants need help to understand where the passages of scripture that are read and the events of everyday life fit into the larger picture of the kingdom. How are we part of the great plan of God? A catechist and pastoral associate from Illinois writes the following:

> The *kerygma* which supports our existence is Love.
> It undergirds all the realities we encounter. So that
> while on one plane life may seem to be full of
> changes—some good, some welcomed, some painful
> and unwelcome—the deeper reality is that all life—
> indeed, all creation—has its source in unconditional
> Love. This Love produces life, wills life, pours
> out life until it spreads out, spills over and saturates
> everything. It is this reality that needs to be grasped
> in order to cope with the unsettling actuality of
> change. Therefore, it is a reality that needs to be
> preached in every changing circumstance, pointing
> to the deeper life-producing Love, showing what
> is really going on. When we preach this, it is an orien-
> tation to deep reality.

In many senses this second aim of mustard seed preaching is not entirely distinct from the first. When we deeply observe and ponder reality, we are moved to wonder and to awe. Wonder and awe aid a falling-in-love. To the degree that mustard seed preachers are successful at penetrating reality for their congregants and setting afire an experience of wonder and awe, they will also have succeeded in helping them to fall in love with the God who created the universe, animates and sustains it, and is bringing it toward the fullness of life.

PREACH THE QUESTIONS

Much of this book has centered on the core human mysteries that are central to children's theology: the mystery of relationship, the mystery of life and death, and the mystery of time. While children wrestle with these mysteries in dialogue with our Christian tradition and find many different images that help them to explore these mysteries, in the end, they remain mysteries. This is because the purpose of mystery in our heritage is not to find a solution, but to entice us into deeper and deeper relationship. The more we know a person, the more time we spend with him or her, the more we discover parts of him or her that we do not understand entirely, and the more we want to know, the more we want to draw near. So it is with God.

Mustard seed theology encourages us to allow mystery to be mystery. The preacher doesn't have to be the one to answer the questions of the congregation, so much as the one to lift them up and invite reflection. The gift of a good question is infinitely more valuable to the congregation than a prefabricated answer. "The Catechesis has taught me the importance of asking open-ended questions in my preaching," states a catechist-priest from Ohio. "When preaching, I never want to shut down the thought process by getting too definitive. If we get too definitive, the congregation exits from the homily." The method of mustard seed theology assumes that everyone in the congregation has the capacity to think and reflect upon important questions, even the smallest.

The value of upholding mystery as mystery in mustard seed theology permits mustard seed preachers the freedom to wonder along with their congregations. It gives them the liberty to stand humbly with their people in the midst of unexplainable joy or sorrow, terrible tragedy or undeserved blessing, and say, "I do not understand the unfathomable depths of life or death, relationship or time either. Let us be in awe together." It allows that reverential silence may sometimes be the best response.

PREACH ESSENTIALLY

The essentiality of the child is a great challenge to preachers. Children have little tolerance for frivolous language, rambling, or esoteric speculation. They insist that our words be concise and well chosen and that our message be vital to their lives. As described earlier, the children ask us for "rich food and not too much of it." Although they may not wiggle in their seats or stand and interrupt like an unengaged child, congregations have a parallel need for rich food in small servings. The approach of mustard seed theology challenges preachers to prepare well for their time in the pulpit and to be clear about what they want to say, since the less certain one is, the more one typically will say. One of the true gifts of mustard seed theology to preachers is that it can help them to discern and lift up what *is* most essential—and hence engaging to congregations—in our Christian Tradition.

PREACH BEAUTIFULLY AND JOYFULLY

Essentiality does not preclude joy and beauty. Rather, joy and beauty are essential for the flourishing of the human spirit. The value that mustard seed theology places on these two qualities challenges preachers to give them a central place in preaching as well. Preachers must ask themselves: Have I found words exquisite enough to express the beauty of the message I proclaim? Does the expression of my body convey the goodness of this message? Do I really believe that what I speak is Good News, or, as the children in the atrium have been prone to say, "Great News"? Such beauty and joy in preaching cannot be contrived simply for the preaching event. While preachers can be intentional about their role in preaching, they are a reflection that the Word has permeated everyday life.

VALUE THE LANGUAGE OF SIGN

The method of mustard seed theology is rooted in the language of sign. Its insights arise out of the innate capacity of children to look at things of the natural world and perceive the supernatural meanings undergirding them. One of the main tasks of the catechist in the atrium is to help children become increasingly aware of the signs that are around them and consciously practice interpreting them. The same could be said of the preacher. True signs do not have one meaning. They have many. When we consciously break open signs in community, we discover the genuine richness of meanings they possess.

When Jesus preached and taught, he always did so in the language of sign. He took objects and events from ordinary life and led people to see the sacred alive in them: mustard seeds, pearls, prodigal sons returning home, sheep being found, bread, wine, water, light. In its liturgical life—of which preaching is an essential part—the Church has preserved Jesus' method. Preaching can help draw attention to and lift up the signs of the Church for reflection, increasing the community's capacity to read through their environment and discover its divine underpinnings. The critical role of sign in our communal life, however, also challenges preachers to be aware of the sign that they are to the assembly. What might they be communicating by their body language, style, dress, and language that they are not aware of? Is the sign of one's person congruent with the message preached?

The above eight points loosely sketch an approach to the ministry of preaching that would be in harmony with the approach that catechists of the Good Shepherd have found particularly effective and meaningful in the ministry of catechesis. These guidelines begin to address the question of *how* mustard seed theology invites preachers to undertake the task of mustard seed preaching. Let us turn now, however, to a second question: *What* does mustard seed theology ask preachers to preach?

What Children Have to Teach Us about Preaching

A Gospel

In the middle chapters of this book, we looked at images and perspectives from the Christian tradition that children have found most helpful in wrestling with the core mysteries of life. In the long course of Sofia's catechetical work, she has introduced children to a large and rich heritage, which they in turn have sifted through. Through their repeated enjoyment of particular themes, the children have lifted up for us what they have discerned to be most essential. In many ways, we could say they have uncovered nothing new. The themes that they have lifted up are the very same themes that the Church has treasured for centuries, the same ones that lay at the heart of our liturgical year. At the same time, the children have helped us rediscover these long-cherished truths from a new perspective and understand the relationship between these truths in exciting new ways. It is as if, to paraphrase the verse of T. S. Eliot, we return to the faith we have practiced since youth and know it for the very first time.[9] In this chapter let us briefly revisit the essential Christian themes that consistently reappear in the Good News as children proclaim it and consider the role these themes play in preaching.

THE KINGDOM OF GOD

In mustard seed theology, the kingdom of God is the ultimate reality, the foundation upon which all else rests. It could be understood as the stage on which the drama of the universe is played out: the law—in essence, the Love—that supports its existence. But it is more than that. It is also the plot line: the movement of "less becoming more" that drives the drama toward its glorious conclusion. Hence, as actors in this drama, we can say not only that we "live and move and have our being" in this kingdom, but also that the kingdom "lives and moves and has its being" within us. The kingdom of God is less a "what" than a "who"—a great and mighty "who" reigning over the universe with a scepter in the shape of a staff, gathering the lost, lifting up the lowly, filling the hungry with good things: A "who" whose power is exercised most magnificently not in violence or majestic force, but in the mystery of growth and transformation.

CREATION

God is love. Love can only exist in the context of relationship. When we say that God is Trinity, we are saying that God's very being is relational. The fruit of relationship is growth and transformation. It is moving from "less to more." It is abundant life. The relationship that *is* God overflowed into the creation of the universe. Creation is a manifestation of the kingdom of God at work. In creation we witness the process of the "less becoming more." We see how out of nothing, God created something. Out of the earliest, most simple forms of life, more and more complex forms of life evolved. Still today, before our very eyes, we can observe this most basic dynamism: in seeds that grow, in the yeast that leavens, in our very own bodies and spirits that began so small and yet continue to grow and change though we "know not how it happens" (Mark 4:27). Creation is a sacrament of the kingdom of God in that it reveals to us who God is and how God works.

God has a dream for creation. God desires that all of creation come to enjoy a fullness of life—the kind of life that exists within God's self—Trinitarian life. Humanity plays a special role in God's dream. Like God, humanity has the capacity to love and to work, to consciously collaborate in the process of growth and transformation. As such, humans have the capacity to enjoy relationship with God in a most particular way. From where humanity stands in time, the history of creation is a history of gifts: the gift of the mineral world, of the plant world, of the animal world, the gift of fellow humans. Through enjoyment of these gifts, the greatness of God's love becomes increasingly apparent to the human person, and the greatness of God's desire to be in relationship with us becomes more known.

INCARNATION

We might think that in the gifts of creation the goodness and generosity of God would be exhausted, but this is not the case. God's desire to be in relationship with us is so immense, that God wanted to give us an even greater gift: the gift of God's very own self, God's very own life, in the person of Jesus Christ. As all things in God's kingdom, the gift of Jesus came shrouded in smallness and hidden-ness. He arrived not on a blazing chariot, but as a tiny ordinary baby. He was born not in Jerusalem, but in Bethlehem. He slept not in a palace, but in a manger. Jesus was like a mustard seed. He was humble and vulnerable, not what we would have expected. But, in his teaching and, moreover, in his person, he showed us that wherever it seems most impossible that God is at work, God is actually about to act the most powerfully.

THE PASCHAL MYSTERY

We know this truth in a most definitive way in the death and Resurrection of Jesus. His Paschal passage is the example par excellence of the kingdom of God at work. As our Good Shepherd, Jesus lived his whole life for his sheep. He wanted to be with them always. He loved them so much that he was willing to die for them. But, he also loved them so much and wanted to be with them so much that he could not remain dead. Even though he lay in the tomb, God raised him from the dead. Where it looked as if no life remained and no life was possible, the most abundant life was about to burst forth. Never again can we say that anything is impossible for God.

BAPTISM AND EUCHARIST

The light and life of the risen Christ is stronger than death. It can never be extinguished again. Through the sacrament of Baptism, we come to share in this light and life. We are initiated into the mystery of the kingdom of God: we receive the flame that gives of itself without losing any of its own radiance; we are washed in the water that can drown, but that paradoxically can also offer new birth; we are anointed with the oils that protect and strengthen the life within us and claim us to be priests, prophets, and royal members of God's reign. We are invited to enjoy our baptismal giftedness each and every day and to continue to grow in Christ's light and life. When we read from scripture, when we pray, when we open and enjoy the gifts of creation, we receive this light and life in ever-greater abundance.

Among the many ways in which the risen Christ is present to us, the Eucharist holds a special place in our hearts. Bread and wine are the signs Jesus chose, on the night before he died, by which he wanted to remain with us until the day when we will see him face to face. He spoke of the bread and wine as his own body and blood—the gift of his whole self to us. When we partake of his body and blood together, we are united ever more deeply to him and to each other.

THE CHRISTIAN LIFE

The gifts of God are abundant. As we become increasingly aware of these gifts, we fall ever more deeply in love with the Giver of the gifts. We are drawn into more intimate relationship. Our first way of responding to the goodness of God is to open the gifts—of creation, of Christ, of sacramental celebration—and revel in them. Our first response is to live joyfully and fully. Our joy is God's joy. "The glory of God," we admit with Irenaeus, "is the human person fully alive."[10] Joy, however, moves toward gratitude and toward the desire to somehow give a gift in response. Since humanity possesses nothing that it has not already received from God, humanity's gift is to offer back to God what God has given, transformed by the work of the human hand. We offer the labors of our body, heart, and mind—whether it be cooking or studying, visiting the imprisoned or sculpting a statue, preaching or filling potholes. Such work, performed in love, furthers the work of the kingdom of God and brings it closer to its fulfillment. Our work is, in fact, an essential part of God's plan. And yet, at the same time, even this work is not entirely our own. We are able to be collaborators with God's plan because we have the Spirit of the risen Christ—Christ's own light and life—coursing through our efforts, like sap runs through the branches of a vine, bringing them to bear much fruit.

THE PAROUSIA

The voice of the Good Shepherd reaches far and wide. Someday all will belong to his flock, all will be branches on his vine, all will be filled with his light and life. Someday God's dream to bring all of creation to a fullness of life will be accomplished. Someday God will be "all in all." We call this day the *parousia*. We do not know when this day will be. Sometimes when we look at the world around us—a world so visibly rife with disharmony and joylessness rather than gratitude and works of love—it seems like it might be a very long time. Then again, when we consider the surprising nature of God's ways, it may be tomorrow. Either way, its coming is promised. We are invited to live in hope, but also with a certain degree of restlessness. It is difficult to wait for something so wonderful—*Maranatha*.

A FRAMEWORK FOR MUSTARD SEED PREACHERS

Mustard seed theology, as discerned by Sofia Cavalletti through her work with children in the Catechesis of the Good Shepherd, is both broad in its scope and rich in substance. In this book, we have only begun to explore the range of children's theological interests and responses that come to light in the atrium. We have sought to lift up only what is most essential among what children have determined is essential. In this brief synthesis of children's core themes in children's theology, however, we have the skeleton that structures and supports the larger body of their theological insight. We have the overarching framework into which their continued learning and reflection fits.

For preachers, having such a framework in mind as they prepare to preach can be very valuable. One of the greatest challenges facing many congregations is the lack of a theological framework. They often possess pieces of the bigger picture—a set of familiar scripture stories, a favorite devotion, knowledge of specific Church teachings or practices— but they miss the links that chain these pieces together and make them into a coherent whole. No one possesses all of the pieces or all of the links, including preachers. But one of the greatest gifts that preachers can offer in their preaching is to help congregations become aware of the bigger picture and the relationship between various themes in our tradition. Scott Appleby, a Church historian, calls this aspect of the preaching ministry "architectonic."[11] Like the style of "bare-bones, nothing-hidden" architecture of the 1970s that this term refers to, he beckons preachers to make explicit the larger structure that supports and unifies the various lections and feasts proclaimed. It means asking questions like the following:

- Where does this story of Abraham (or Moses or Mary) fit into the bigger picture of God's plan for all of creation?

- What does this particular infancy narrative reveal to us about the way that God's kingdom works?

- How do we understand this particular event in our lives differently because of the death and Resurrection of Christ?

- How is the daily work of our hands part of God's work?

- How does this reading help us to better understand what it means to be baptized or to share in the Eucharistic feast?

- Why are we reading about the *parousia* during the season of Advent when we remember the Incarnation of Christ? How are these two events related?

- How does this letter of Paul help us to understand the Paschal Mystery better? The *parousia?*

- How does our belief in the Trinity affect the way we live in relationship?

When preaching wrestles with such questions, it illumines the framework of our faith and encourages congregants to draw vivid connections between their life stories and God's story. No longer are their experiences perceived as isolated or random events in time. They are anchored in a grand plot line—the next chapter of which is unknown, but the end of which has already been written. They are oriented toward the larger, ultimate reality.

CONCLUSION

There is a story well circulated among catechists of the Good Shepherd concerning Pope John Paul II's visit to an atrium in the parish of Nostra Signora Di Lourdes in Rome. During his time there, the pope was said to move from table to table watching the children work intently with the materials. Sometimes, he would stop and ask various groups of children questions as they worked, pausing to listen to their reflection. At the close of the atrium session, the pope turned to the catechists and stated, "I have never heard such a beautiful homily."[12]

I sometimes wonder what it was exactly that the revered bishop heard. This was a man who had heard thousands of homilies in his lifetime—spoken in numerous languages and by some of the most learned and charismatic preachers on the planet. But, among the young children at work, he heard the Christian message proclaimed in a way that he had not heard before—a way that moved him deeply. Was it the insight of one child that he was referring to? The compilation of observations children made on this particular day? Or was it simply the model of children and adults listening together before the Word of God? We do not know. But, he received it as a most "beautiful homily."

The encounter at Nostra Signora di Lourdes is for me an image of the dynamic that this book has sought to serve. It is an image of the Church listening to and with its youngest members. It is an image of the Church hearing the Gospel it preaches anew through the lens of the little. It is an image of the Church falling more deeply in love with its God via the voice of a child. My hope is that these pages have captured something of what the pope heard that day, and that—if they have done justice to the mustard seed theology of the child— they will have been experienced as a "beautiful homily,"the kind of homily that gives hope and encouragement to the mustard seed preacher.

The kingdom of God *is* in our midst. It comes like a mustard seed, almost invisible to the human eye. It comes like a baby asleep in a manger. It comes like the dawn on the first day of the week. It comes like a child with a question in mind. It comes like a word spoken humbly and joyfully in faith—a word barely audible over sneezes and hungry toddlers and the ever-present bells and whistles of contemporary culture. But a word that might change . . . *that will change* the world.

SAMPLES OF MUSTARD SEED PREACHING

It is one thing to describe what my own preaching looks like. It is another to translate the ideas presented in this book into an actual homily or reflection for a liturgical assembly. In the pages that follow, I humbly offer four samples of mustard seed preaching as examples of how the approach and content described in this book might take concrete form. These samples were preached in the context of community prayer at Aquinas Institute and St. Pius V parish in St. Louis.

READING: MATTHEW 4:13—17

Last Sunday we celebrated the Baptism of the Lord. The feast seems to serve as a bridge between the Christmas season that we are wrapping up and the Ordinary Time that we are beginning. In thinking about this over the past week, I began to reflect that the feast points us as much forward to what is coming as it points back to the season from which it came, . . . and that continued meditation on its Gospel might be a good thing at the beginning of this new semester.

Meeting Jesus in the infancy narratives that we have heard during the Christmas season presents us with a great paradox. He is born an ordinary baby, and yet angels announce his birth. He is laid in a manger amidst beasts of burden, yet the stars of the sky cradle him with light. He is found amidst lowly shepherds, yet kings bring him gifts. His parents are so poor they bring only turtle doves to his consecration in the temple, but they are welcomed by prophets.

They give him a most common name: *Jesus.* But, in the readings of the last several weeks, we've heard him called

Ruler of the House of Jacob

Heir of the Throne of David

Emmanuel

Messiah and Lord

The Word Made Flesh

The Light of the Gentiles

The Glory of Israel

Prince

Shepherd of God's People

Now, today, we hear one last name. One last key to unlocking this man's identity.

We have heard who he is to us. Now, we hear who he is to God.

He is *Beloved.* He is *Son.*

Names are interesting things. It is always an interesting conversation to debate the power of a name. We always say that we are not the same as our names, that what people call us doesn't really matter. But, would my life be radically different if—from birth—my parents had named me Colleen (as my dad had advocated) instead of Ann? Or if they had named me Muffy or Zoe? All are fine names, but would I have become someone different from who I am? Perhaps. We certainly continue to become more aware of the effects of name-calling on the self-esteem of children—how the label "Stupid" can haunt a person long after it is last applied. Names do shape us in a mysterious way as we become what we are called.

Many of the names attributed to Jesus in the infancy narratives we have focused on so prominently in the last few weeks, we know, were probably applied to him after he had died and risen. These infancy narratives were the last parts of the Gospels written—the fruit of much reflection by various disciples about the true identity of this man in their midst. They were applied by others to describe the Jesus they had experienced. Our Gospel today, however, gives us insight into how Jesus possibly experienced himself as named.

The event of Jesus' baptism by John is one of only a handful of stories that all four of the Gospels have in common. While each Gospel tells it slightly different, by its frequency we must be convinced of its powerful and formative effect on Jesus' life. Matthew and Mark lead us to believe that Jesus himself was the source of the story. For it is only Jesus who sees the sky rent in two and the Spirit descending like a dove. And, in the Gospel of Mark (the earliest of the Christian Gospels), it is only Jesus who hears the voice: "You are my beloved Son. On you my favor rests." While the Christian community would come to affirm this divine naming, we might guess that it began as his own spiritual insight that he shared with those closest to him.

Of all the names we have heard given to Jesus over the last couple of weeks, this alone seems to be the one he heard himself. The one that whispered and boomed and echoed throughout his entire life. The one that shaped his whole person. The one that formed him into who he would become. "You are my beloved son."

Would Jesus have been Jesus without this name? Without this knowledge? We can speculate "no." The infancy narratives reveal several "epiphany" events in which Christ's true identity was made known to others. The story of Christ's baptism seems to reveal the "epiphany" event in which Jesus' true identity became known to himself. "I am the beloved son of God."

We can imagine how this knowledge must have made him feel—the joy, the kind of tickle in the gut when one knows that one is the object of infatuation, of affection. We can imagine how the world looked more beautiful to Jesus—how the sun shone brighter, how the birds sang more sweetly, how the flowers bloomed more radiantly—on the morning after his baptism. *"I am beloved."* We can imagine how people became friendlier, power figures less intimidating, hardship less frightening. *"I am beloved."*

Jesus' baptism shaped his whole world view. It affected everything: the work he would take on, the way he interacted with people, what he preached . . . and eventually the way he would die. The knowledge of his "beloved-ness," his "sonship" gave him the courage and the conviction to pick up the cross, kept him faithful to the end. *This* was the man—the beloved one—that God raised from the dead. And *Beloved* is the name, above all other names, that led us to calling upon him by so many names.

It is not his name alone, however. For, in Baptism, each one of us was called "Beloved" by God. Each one of us was called "Child." For each one of us the sky is rent and the Spirit descends. But have you heard yet? You have come out of the water, but have you heard? Do you have a tickle in your gut knowing that the divine smiles down on you with affection, . . . delights in your very being? . . . Do you really know?

And are you letting this love form you? Is it shaping the way that you look at the world? Is it determining your every activity, your every interaction? . . . Is it giving you courage? Is it giving you hope? . . . And, is it giving you strength to pick up that cross, to stare death in the eye, and to know that God's faithfulness is always vindicated in resurrection?

When we speak about the change of liturgical colors with the children in the atrium, we speak about green as the "growing time" that follows the "festal" white time. It is the time in which we let the "joy of the feast grow in our hearts." As we enter into "green time" this week, it seems particularly fitting to continue to revel in this last great epiphany of the season of epiphanies. As we begin this new semester, before we drown in the demands about to be set upon us, let us share a few moments of silence this week to allow God to look at us with affection, as on the day of our Baptism . . . and to hear the name that shapes us, the name that most "becomes" us, the name that gives reason for everything we are about to do.

READING: LUKE 1:26—38

The history of Israel begins with a woman named Sarah and her wandering husband Abraham who follows directions no one else hears—the commands of an unknown God with dubious powers, only promises. It begins with a triad of visitors in the heat of the day who speak with one voice, and make the most fantastic promise yet—a long-desired son unsealing the womb of the long-barren Sarah, her child-bearing years long past. It begins with a hearty laugh and a question (that sounds perhaps more like a dare): "Is *anything* impossible for the Lord?"

Is anything impossible for the Lord?

It is a question that ricochets throughout Israel's
    history.
Cresting on the waves of the Red Sea.
Whistling through the sand hills of the Sinai desert
    coated with a thin crust of manna.
Thundering as the walls of Jericho tumbled and fire
    rained down on the drenched offering of Elijah
Hummed in the lullabyes of Hannah
Shouted with glee as Goliath's body hit the ground
    with a thud. . . .
And Judith returned with the dripping head of
    Holofernes.

Is anything impossible for the Lord?
Cyrus, the mysterious Persian, emerges from nowhere
    to end an endless exile.
Lamps with oil for one night remain lit for eight.
Water spurts from rocks.

Donkeys talk.
Men sleep with lions and sing in furnaces
To the echoing refrain of Miriam's tamborine.

Is anything impossible for the Lord?

In the course of *time,* Israel saw its unknown God of promises step out of the shadows to respond to Sarah's dare— slowly moving from unknown toward known, from promise toward action, from un-carnate toward incarnate.

Month by month,
year by year,
century by century,
everyday life punctuated rhythmically by a series of
        most unlikely events—
A melody line unfolding, though sometimes lost
        amidst the other
cacophonous patterns of history, equally intricate.
Crescendo-ing unto the heat of that day
        in the tiny village of Nazareth,
when to Sarah's most distant daughter was given—
        once and for all—heaven's definitive answer:
A great resounding, "No!" from the mouth of Gabriel,
        "No. Nothing is impossible with God."

And, you, Mary, shall carry within you God's final answer—given in the form of a child, whose whole existence will be a paradox—an impossibility from the beginning all the way unto the end.

This day—March 25—deep in the heart of Lent, we celebrate the feast of the Annunciation, the feast of God's great definitive announcement in Christ. It seems like such a strange feast to mark at this time of year when our focus is tilted toward the end of Jesus' life rather than its beginning. It almost feels artificially placed nine months before Christmas Day, a far flung star from the constellation of Incarnation feasts that just happens to cross lines with the Paschal Mystery constellation. And yet, for the original Jewish Christians, such intersection was not incidental.

Ancient Jewish custom assumed that great persons were conceived and died on the same date, and there is some evidence that possibly the feast of the Annunciation preceded the feast of Christmas as an established celebration in the earliest centuries of the Church, because it was the date reckoned to be the original Good Friday. We might think this custom to be pure folklore occasioned by rare coincidence, but my suspicion is that the belief captures a deeper intuition that there is a profound connection between our birth and our death—a certain oneness and consistency to our person from beginning to end.

When we celebrate the Annunciation in the midst of Lent, we recognize that the virgin birth of Christ and the death and Resurrection of Christ are not two separate mysteries, but facets of the one same mystery—one same answer.

A one-chord climax to the golden melody line of history:

Nothing. Nothing is impossible for your God.

Still the air vibrates with this chord as it lingers, trembling. One strong, pure harmony of pitches ringing out.

Children of Sarah, can you hear it over the din?
The orchestra is entering into its finale.
There are cymbals crashing everywhere.

Competing melodies rise and fall wailing.

God does not care.

God is uninvolved in human history.

God is dead.

God does not hear your prayers.

Can you still hear God's great announcement of this day?
Listen.
In these dark days, listen carefully.
And, if it helps you in your struggle to hear,
know that this chord is accompanied by the sound of
a hearty laugh.
This is not the laugh of Sarah you are hearing.
This is the last laugh—
the one that belongs to God.

In our first reading today, from Revelation, John describes for us a vision—a vision that he has had of the communion of saints. He describes seeing thousands upon thousands of women and men from every nation and race and tongue processing before the throne of God. They are bathed in white; basking in the presence of the Lamb of God, Jesus Christ.

In our own imagination, we can easily embellish John's description with the varieties of saints that we have heard of since childhood: Great missionaries like Paul or Francis Xavier who preached the Good News to the ends of the earth, the martyrs like Cecelia or Agnes who gave their lives for their faith. We might envision the great reformers like Teresa of Avila or Charles Borromeo rubbing shoulders with the holy popes like Pius the Fifth or with simple folk like Therese of Liseux who did ordinary things well. Tossed in amid the brilliant scholars like Thomas Aquinas would be those considered by their contemporaries to be mentally lacking, like Germaine, or real eccentrics, like Simon the Stylite who spent 40 years of his life atop a tall pillar. Some would have spent their lives in the royal courts, like Charles Lwanga or Thomas More. And some would have never had a roof over their heads, like Francis of Assisi. From every corner of the earth, we can see these holy souls—this walking litany—converging with grandeur upon the sanctuary of heaven, singing praise to God.

Such a fantastic vision John had! Such beauty he witnessed! Almost too good to be true.

But, you know what? I, too, have had a vision very similar to John's. And, I wasn't in a trance. I didn't have to eat any scrolls or have my lips singed by burning coals. But I, too, have seen a people of every nation garbed in white, basking in the presence of the Lamb of God. Some of them possessing great courage. Some of them giving their lives for their beliefs. Some great reformers. Some simple and ordinary, but nonetheless holy. Some rich. Some poor. Some, quite frankly, a little on the strange side. Some brilliant, some mentally disabled. I've seen this great procession of the multitudes praising God in song.

Such a vision. Such a beauty. Almost too good to be true.

And, I expect to see it again today in about, say, 20 minutes. It is the St. Pius communion line.

"How can this be?" some may ask. We become saints only when we enter into our eternal life. This is true. But, when does our eternal life begin? At death? That is not what our scriptures and our Catholic tradition tell us. We enter into eternal life when we enter into relationship with God, the Source of All Life, at Baptism.

It is at our Baptism that we are initiated into the Paschal Mystery. It is at our Baptism that we are washed clean by the blood of the Lamb. It is at our Baptism that we receive our white garments, our robes of eternal life. And, ever so slowly, it is from the baptismal font that we are nudged into that grand procession toward the Eucharistic table to enjoy Christ's presence in the bread and the cup of immortality.

We have already entered into our eternal life. Once, you were strangers or aliens, Paul writes to the Ephesians, but now you are saints—saints in the house of God. Once you were nobodies, the first letter of John records, but "dearly beloved, we are God's children now." Once you were considered only "poor in spirit," records Matthew's Gospel, but really the "reign of God is yours."

Such a vision. Such a beauty. Almost too good to be true.

This is not to deny, of course, the presence of sin and failing in our midst. We are painfully aware that our communion with God and with each other is incomplete. We are still wracked by disagreements and shortcomings. Times of trial still test our resolve. Our love is yet imperfect. We have not yet even come close to realizing fully who we are to become as a people. Perhaps when we hear the beatitudes now, we can only identify with the sorrowing, the meekness, the suffering and persecution. We do not see how these could possibly be signs of our blessedness, our righteousness, our progress toward sanctity. We think of our lives here as radically discontinuous with the next. This is earth. That is heaven. This is us. That is them.

But, in the coming of Jesus Christ—both true God and true human—there is no longer a radical break between heaven and earth. Between the holy and the mundane. Between the other-worldly and the this-worldly. There is only one communion of saints and it bridges the chasm of death to embrace both here and there.

Perhaps it is best to think of ourselves as mustard seed saints. We cannot tell by looking at the seed what the tree will look like in its maturity. A tree is something very different than a seed. But, everything that the tree will become is already locked inside that seed. Every bud contains all that will blossom. And everything that we will become—all of our potential, in fact eternal life itself—is already budding inside of us.

Let us pray that this communion we process toward today may nourish our budding sainthood. May it reconcile us once more in the blood of the Lamb. May it draw us into closer relationship with God, into deeper communion with all the saints. May we experience heaven, right here today.

Such a vision. Such a beauty. Almost too good to be true.

READING: MARK 9:30—37

When Micah was just a little over a year old, maybe a year and a half, one night I had the radical idea that maybe I should start praying with him . . . you know, being a theology student and all. In some of my own studies, I had been reading about the child's innate relationship with God that longed to have a space to express itself. So, I sat down on his mattress on the floor as he lay down to go to sleep at night and I said to him, "Micah, is there anything you'd like to say to Jesus before you go to sleep tonight?" Now mind you the kid hardly spoke more than 20 words at this point and I wasn't sure he was even going to know what I was talking about. But, he just kind of looked beyond me and said, very clearly and very intentionally, "Alleluia."

When we listen to language as it first emerges from the mouths of babes—if we listen very carefully—we will hear the primordial words of our faith.

The earliest words are always the most important, and so it begins with the joyful, "Abababababa . . ." for hours on end while rolling across the living room floor. In the exercising of the tongue, the most intimate name for God that we have known in human history—the one which we waited centuries for—to the insult of the dignified—naturally rolls off the lips of the five-month-old.

And it is only a matter of time—and a few consonants—until we hear "allelelele" over and over again. From God's name to God's praise. Are these words created by us? Or are we created for these words? Have we chosen them to address God, or have they chosen us? So close to our hearts, so close to our origins, are these words that it seems predestined that in our mastery of human language we should need to utter them.

Alleluia—the primordial expression of praise. The first prayer of all of us.

Today, as we prepare to enter into the season of Lent, we take pause to lift up this precious word, "Alleluia." For, during Lent, it is taken from us. Our first joy, our first prayer is taken from us, to be buried like a seed. Not as a punishment—though it may feel like that—but so that in abstinence, our heart may remember our fondness, our natural inclination for the word that springs from our innermost being and rolls from our lips. We bury it like a seed so that it might grow—so that the spirit of praise will take root again in our lives and blossom with the spring.

We bury it like a seed so that at the crack of dawn, six weeks from now, we will recognize it once again as the *first* song of an Easter people.

NOTES

1. Tina Lillig, *The Catechesis of the Good Shepherd in a Parish Setting* (Chicago: Liturgy Training Publications, 1998), 6. In addition to this text, the biographical and historical information in this chapter comes from: Jerome W. Berryman, "Montessori Religious Education: Sofia Cavalletti (1917–)," *PACE* 23 (May 1994), 3–7; and, Sofia Cavalletti, et al., *The Good Shepherd and the Child: A Joyful Journey* (New Rochelle, NY: Don Bosco Multimedia, 1994), 89–100.

2. Sofia Cavalletti, *The Religious Potential of the Child: Experiencing Scripture and Liturgy with Children* (Chicago: Liturgy Training Publications, 1992), 140.

3. Augustine of Hippo, *The Confessions of St. Augustine in The Nicene and Post-Nicene Fathers, vol. 1,* ed. Philip Schaff (Grand Rapids, MI: Eerdmans, 1956), sec. 1.

4. Sofia Cavalletti. *The Religious Potential of the Child: Experiencing Scripture and Liturgy with Young Children* (Chicago: Liturgy Training Publications, 1992), 141.

5. Sofia Cavalletti, *The Religious Potential of the Child 6 to 12 Years Old* (Chicago, Liturgy Training Publications, 2002), 6.

6. Sofia Cavalletti, *Religious Potential of the Child: Experiencing Scripture and Liturgy with Young Children* (Chicago: Liturgy Training Publications, 1992), 176.

7. Sofia Cavalletti, *History's Golden Thread: the History of Salvation* (Chicago: Liturgy Training Publications, 1999), 21.

8. Karl Rahner, "Ideas for a Theology of Childhood," *Theological Investigations,* vol. 8, trans. David Bourke. (New York: Herder, 1971), 36.

9. T. S. Eliot, "Four Quartets" in Julia Maniates Reibetanz, *A Reading of Eliot's Four Quartets* (Ann Arbor, MI: UMI Research Press, 1983), 183.

10. Ireneaus, *Against Heresies, in The Ante-Nicene Fathers: The Apostolic Fathers with Justin Martyr and Irenaeus,* vol. 1, ed. James Donaldson and Alexander Roberts (Grand Rapids, MI: Eerdmans, 1951), sec. 4.20.7.

11. Scott Appleby, "Critical Issues Facing Theological Education in the United States," Aquinas Institute of Theology Faculty Retreat, St. Louis, Missouri, January 7, 2003.

12. Sofia Cavalletti, private e-mail to Patricia Stenton, February 7, 2003. The event is also referenced in a letter by Tilde Camosso Cocchini in *Journals of the Catechesis of the Good Shepherd, 1984–1997,* ed. Victoria M. Tufano (Chicago: Liturgy Training Publications, 1998), 131.